Interdimensional Traveller

DL Williams

Burning Eye

Interdimensional Traveller

This QR code will lead you to the Interdimensional Traveller Youtube channel which accompanies this book. It can also be found at:
https://www.youtube.com/channel/
UCwN8uH7LHHLVEyKq2NUg66Q

Other QR codes included in the book link directly to films of the poems they follow.

CONTENTS

DL Williams is a deaf queer poet working with British Sign Language and English. Working with such different languages has inspired a deep interest in translation and how her work can be made accessible to signing and non-signing audiences. They have performed around the UK including at the Scottish Storytelling Centre, Wales Millennium Centre, the Barbican and the Albert Hall, as well as in America and Brazil. She has most recently been published in 'What Meets the Eye?' an anthology of deaf poets (2021) and Modern Poetry in Translation (2022). Their poems cover many themes, from identity to bilingualism to their beloved cats and as she says: "I aim to make my work accessible to everyone; whether you enjoy it or not is another matter!"

WHO AM I? (Written 2006)

<pre>
                    Who am I?
Raised in hearing culture
                            Late… found deaf culture
Hearing identity have
                                Deaf identity have
                Both absorbed
        But they grind and fracture

                    Who am I?
In the hearing world
I'm labelled 'hearing-impaired'
'Broken'… 'damaged'
                                    In the Deaf world
                            I'm labelled 'speaks well'
                                'Half-hearing'… 'oral'

I can speak
But do I fit in the hearing world?
Sometimes…
                                        I can sign
                        But do I fit in the Deaf world?
                                    Sometimes…

Half-hearing

                                Half-deaf
        Together becomes what?
            Who am I?
</pre>

THE APPLE

Once upon a time
there was a beautiful garden,
a verdant forest,
and in the sea of green
a special tree towered
with a very special fruit
guarded by a serpent
entwined in the branches,
watching,
waiting
for unsuspecting prey…

    Tempting.

        Refraining.
        (They said I shouldn't.)

    Persuading.

        Resisting.
        (They really said I shouldn't.)

    Seducing.

        Resistance fades, crumbles.
        The apple, devoured.
        Ravenous enjoyment.

But wait…

        The fruit is absorbed.
        The juices effervesce.
        The energy spreads.

        Sign Language is gained
        and knowledge enlightens!

THE DUCKLING AND THE DISSERTATION

Dissertation deadline coming fast,
panic seizing my heart.
Panicpanicpanicpanicpanic.

Books and laptop arrayed,
fingers type till they're frayed.
Typetypetypetypetype.

Enough! There's a park somewhere.
I need a walk, some fresh air.
Walkwalkwalkwalkwalk.

A swollen river with rushing rapids,
a duckling paddling, battling the current.
Paddlepaddlepaddlepaddlepaddle.

In that moment,
a metaphysical connection.

BELLA'S PENGUINS

I feel like a penguin

Water

Land

Fish
Can in water
Smooth, fluid, beautiful

But can't on land
Flapping uselessly

Cats
Mewling away

But can't in water
They flounder

Penguins

Smooth in water

Can on land
But they stumble

But still can both
I feel like a penguin

Can dive in water

Can waddle on land
Or lie on the beach
Dream of space!

With thanks to Dr Donna West, a sign language researcher, and the original Bella.

THAT DAY

That day when I am no longer pushed aside because I
didn't hear someone say 'excuse me',

that day when all information is put on screens instead of
bellowed over tannoys,

that day when I am no longer patronised; 'CAN YOU
LIPREAD?'

that day when job adverts don't say 'must have good
telephone manner',

that day when all children are taught to sign,

that day when telephone helplines are thrown away and
replaced by visual conferencing,

that day when I can snap my fingers and find an
interpreter,

that day when society becomes fully deaf-aware,

that day…

I will stop claiming DLA.

*DLA stands for Disability Living Allowance, now known as
Personal Independence Payment or PIP.*

BILINGUAL POET'S DILEMMA

Published online as BSL poem with captions at Scottish Poetry Library. Video directed by Sandra Alland and filmed by Ania Urbanowska.

As I hunt for inspiration,
for poetry revelation,
I wonder, if it's in Sign,
how to make it rhyme.
No sign has seventeen phonemes,
and how to count the cheremes?
And how to write the lines
of all the different signs?
And just how does one
write a signed pun?
I could use special notations,
but that would require more patience;
I could scribble some notes,
but that's not very poetic – boats!
I can wave my hands in air,
but that's not a rhyming pair,
and that's before I consider
iambic pentameter;
     wherefore art thou absent, inspiring muse?
     Why dost thou not appear in time of need?
     Have I not shown you dedication? O,
     enticing one, when shall I beauty see?
Don't mind if it's in Sign
or words in witty lines;
all I really want
is a poetry detente
where, when I'm inspired,
I can think of words required,
or Signs that can express,
or images undress,

but not so they conflict
and leave me feeling tricked.
What's beautiful in a Sign
is boring in a line;
what's pretty in a line
is confusing in Sign,
and if the twain should meet,
wouldn't that be a feat?
So tell me, please,
which language should I use?
Which one should I choose?

DEAF

Different
in a world of sound.
In my difference,
beauty I've found.

Extraordinary:
strange, weird, odd, rude, stupid, blunt, slow, ignorant, dumb,
inspiring, thick, special, visual, physical, unusual…
Terms may vary,
but I will never be ordinary.

Alter,
sidelined in 2D planes.
Within three dimensions
you'll find my domain.

Fluid,
negotiating between worlds.
My language, my hands, my signs
free me from confines.

I am *DEAF.*

FINALLY, A DREAM COME TRUE

*Inspired by Doctor Who: a tribute to the Doctor and
Cass. Filmed by Martin Haswell.*

He's met just about everyone;
he's wandered time and space.
He's met the Face of Boe
and the Boe's original face.

He's met kings, queens and emperors
and defeated quite a few.
He's met cults, supremes, hybrids,
enemies old and new.

He's met the distant descendants
of lizards, bugs and cats.
He's met plastic Santas
and younglings made of fat.

He's met the transcorporeals,
the upgraded, downloaded, enhanced.
He's met the wilfully evil
and the hopelessly entranced.

He's bumbled around the twisting, turning
timeline of his life.
He's tangled with erratic psychopaths;
he's met his future wife.

He's met the barely living,
he's met the really dead.
But after aeons of travelling
he's finally met the deaf!

ISN'T THIS ART?

There are cave paintings in France,
pictures that speak at a glance
of mammoths in ancient times
and others time left behind.

Is this art?

Celtic warriors in blue,
modern tribal tattoos,
images on the skin
revealing thoughts within.

Is this art?

What of statues unmoving?
Pictures made of stone
or ice, or wood, or anything;
lifeless, blank-faced drones.

Is this art?

Paintings hung for years,
faded by time and eyes.
Old paint and new meanings,
worth more if the artist dies.

Is this art?

Graffiti colourfully sprayed,
images, tags and phrases
wherever the artist fancies,
attracting various gazes.

Is this art?

Photos of beauty and power,
pictures of some moment chosen.
2D, flat, motionless:
images forever frozen.

Is this art?

Poetry of pen and page,
words picked with greatest care.
Obsessing down to a comma;
to put something here or there.

Is this art?

Tapestries painstakingly woven,
thread upon thread upon thread,
until someone goes blind or mad
and all the subjects dead.

Is this art?

And what of signs of hands?
Pictures weaved in air,
beguiling an audience entranced,
a poet's imagination shared.

Isn't this art?

THE EMPTY TABLE

Published online as BSL poem with captions for 'Fly the Flag' in recognition of Article 25 of the Universal Declaration of Human Rights.

A table of every colour and hue,
surrounded by people, laden with food,
unfortunately subjected to autocratic rule.
Taking offence
    Is your race different from mine?

            Get out!

for one reason
     What religion are you?

            Get out!

or another,
      Are you disabled?

            Get out!

       valid or invalid,
fair or not,
      Are you queer?

            Get out!

    Are you a mother? Is that your child?
     Where's your husband?

            Get out!

logical or not;
     Hey, you – do you have a job?

            Get out!

they fear the other.
     Did you just cough? Are you sick?

            Get out!

    Are you deaf? CAN YOU HEAR ME?

Get out!

What did you say?! YOU ARE SO WRONG!

Get out!

Until eventually…
There's no one left.
No one to bring food, no one to share.
No winners
anywhere.

A TWO-WAY STREET

Communication   Commun----------ication   Communication
Communication   Commun----
Communication breakdown

THESE HANDS ARE WIDER THAN THE SKY

Inspired by Emily Dickinson's 'The Brain Is Wider Than the Sky'.

These hands are wider than the sky;
the sky they contain.
The sun and planets and moon and stars
and more, they sustain.

These hands are deeper than the sea;
the meaning they portray
goes far beyond what you can see,
as all things they convey.

These hands are just the same as sound,
for judge them, line by sign,
and they will differ, if they do,
in how they touch the mind.

THIS FEN DIGRAM (AUTO-CAPTIONED)

A digram: a sequence of two adjacent letters or symbols.

This fen digram
maize little says.
No won utter stands
why the lies are draw this way.
Why musk the battle be for hear
and not the air?
Yews of eerie,
degrease of deaf,
worlds of cray.
Why nora ray bow
fall of bright cars
in dead of these
nonsense call lies?

This Venn diagram
makes little sense.
No one understands
why the lines are drawn this way.
Why must the battle be fought here
and not there?
Hues of hearing,
degrees of deaf,
swirls of grey.
Why not a rainbow,
full of bright colours
instead of these
nonsensical lines?

I HAVE A HEARING RELATIVE JUST LIKE YOU

I have a hearing relative just like you;
it's amazing,
honestly.
You'd almost believe they were normal.

They can hear so much –
it must be so distracting!
Yet you deal with it –
you're such an inspiration.

I can't imagine being hearing,
all that clamour and commotion.
It must be simply awful –
a constant aggravation.

Phones ringing, cars rumbling,
dogs barking, toilets flushing,
mowers roaring, bodies grumbling,
choppers whirring, water rushing –
how on Earth do you get any peace?

You're amazing, so inspiring.
I wish I could be so brave.
Just like my hearing relative.
Just like you.

RECIPE FOR CREATION

Take a human brain
and a smidgen of inspiration.
Add some necessity.
Blend with desperation.
Sprinkle with sweat and
scatter with tears.
Fold in some swear words (if desired).
Bake under high pressure.
Test for doneness.
Finally, garnish with courage; be careful!
This is a rare and precious ingredient.
Serve your creation to the masses and step back.

RECIPE FOR A POEM

Take an idea,
melt it down until simmering.
Carefully stir in some thought.
Sprinkle in some ink.
Heat until notes have started to form and brown.
Fold in some flights of fancy.
Some optional ingredients can be added at this point if
desired
(onomatopoeia, rhyming pairs, analogy).
Mix until well blended
and the poem has absorbed all the flavours.
Garnish with a flourish of voice, of hand.
Serve on a stage and enjoy.

THE DEAF INTERVIEW

Why don't we start with your name?
Fairly common – not related to anyone we might know?

Where are you from?
Oh, so do you know X, Y or Z? …No?

What school did you attend?
Mainstream? I see.

Mother, father deaf?
Your mother? Excellent!

But she doesn't sign?
Oh, I see.

So, raised oral or sign?
Aha. So you speak well…?

Yes, we suspected your English might be quite good.
By the way, is that an implant we see?

Yes, well.
We'll let you know.

3D SEASONS

In my language,
spring literally blooms from my palm,
the summer sun shines from my fingers,
while autumn leaves drift lazily downwards
before the clenched chills of winter.

IF CATS JUDGED CATS

Some say cats are like people;
I wouldn't insult them like that.
They certainly know their own mind,
but I've never seen a cat judge a cat.

Never seen a Scottish fold
point and call a sphynx bald
and laugh at its lack of fur.

Nor an Abyssinian
mock a Himalayan
for the funny sound of its purr.

Never seen a tuxedo
deride an albino
or a rex push a Manx in a puddle.

Or a mau acting haughty
and teasing a tortie
because their mottles were a muddle.

Never seen a moggie tease
a posh Siamese
for looking like an aristocrat.

And would it do
if a Russian blue
called a Maine coon fat?

Ever seen a Burmese
go up to a Tonkinese
and take the piss out of their name?

Never mind a ragamuffin
or a bobtail or a munchkin;
to a cat, it's all the same.

So I wouldn't say cats are like people;
I think cats are smarter than that.
They might be highborn or feral,
but to a cat, a cat is a cat.

CAPTIVATED BY…

Inspired by Doctor Who.

Once upon a time,
before mobiles, emails or streaming
had even been dreamed of,
when we had VHS
and we needed caption decoders
hooked up with cables,
in the dark ages,
I saw a beacon of light.
I was a young thing, strolling past the TV,
when I saw…
whoosh!
A blue box bouncing side to side
in a swirling vortex.
Ooh, looks interesting… nah.
Wait!
What's that?
It has subtitles!
I'm drawn in…
Cybermen!
Daleks!
Silurians!
Davros!
New planets, different worlds,
history made anew!
A spaceship bigger than you think,
time and space,
wibbly wobbly timey wimey.
A young Whovian,
completely captivated.
Not by the Doctor…
by the subtitles!

MY CASTLE

I imagine
that my home is my castle.
It's where I feel safe;
it has walls,
though the bricks are DVDs and books.
The heating is less traditional,
wood and flames superseded by dials and buttons.
Unclean, cold surrounding moat is now
lovely, warm, cleansing surrounding bubbles.
The drawbridge swings sideways instead of down;
I open it to welcome friends.
One of the most important parts of any castle
is the kitchen.
No spits going round and round;
here, things are stirred round and round a pan,
on a hob instead of on a fire.
I raise the flag:
a rainbow of many hues,
emblazoned with glasses and hearing aids,
cats rampant.
My home is my castle.

CONVERSATION DOA

Please don't take this personally,
but I think you might be dead.
For all that you're trying to talk to me,
I've no idea what you said.

You're just not moving at all;
the only sign of life is your eyes.
I'm sure you're trying to communicate,
but all I can see are your sighs.

Why can't you just move your mouth?
Use your face and hands to express.
Move your lips up and down.
Instead you're making me guess.

It's like talking to a waxwork doll.
I'd be better off at Madame Tussauds,
or striking up a conversation
with a smiling advertising board.

Why are you treating me like it's my fault?
You're the one who needs medical aid.
Stop glaring at me like that;
you're not the only one who's getting frayed.

Just move your face! Open your mouth,
let me see your teeth,
talk like you're trying to communicate,
let me see the meaning beneath.

I'm not saying you should patronise me
with exaggerated goldfish impressions.
I'm not asking for facial gymnastics;
just for some facial expressions.

A curse on the stiff upper lip.
You should look in a mirror sometime.
What's the point of lips that don't move?
Try it: can you read a straight line?

Just get some paper and pen;
you're gonna have to write this down.
And kindly don't pout like that;
do you think I can't see your frown?

It's time to pronounce this conversation.
Can someone call the coroner, please?
Maybe when you learn sign language,
we can communicate with ease.

RED AND GREEN

A chest infection,
feverish delirium;
a flight of imagination.
Are you ready to rumble?
In the red corner, the immune system!
In the green corner, the invading virus!
Ring that bell!
Oh, it's a tussle –
green corner using some underhanded tactics,
and oh dear, the red corner doesn't know what to do!
Seconds out…
Red corner receiving treatment,
here we go.
Oh dear me, red seems keen
but green is all over it!
This looks like a knockout is coming!
Seconds out…
Ooh, the red coach is not happy;
some new treatment here.
Well, I say,
whatever the red coach did seems to have worked;
red's looking good!
Green putting up a fight,
but red has the measure of him now!
We have a winner!
Red lifts the trophy
and green is thrown out of the ring
and away.

ON A BRIDGE

Standing on a bridge.
Far below,
hoots of encouragement,
of annoyance.

Going to work,
rushing for a date.
Wouldn't it be terrible
if everyone was late?

In the end,
only one was late.

Inspired by a local news story of a suicidal man who was on a motorway bridge while cars below hooted and people told him to get on with it and jump. Eventually, he did.

PHOENIX GARDEN

Translation to English by Dr Kyra Pollitt, with thanks to an earlier translation by Dr Donna West.

A long time ago,
in a garden,
blades of grass
painted neat, tidy strokes;
flower brights splashed
here and there and here.

Trees gently bowing
to a butterfly's polka
as it pauses,
fans its wings,
whirls on.

A buzzing
(or is there something wrong with my hearing aid?).
It's a bee,
hovering, pollen-dusting,
now busying along.

The birds practise their harmonies
as I gaze on.

Later, I must leave and
another takes my place,
fag in mouth,
rummaging for matches
in dark pockets.
A strike.
A light.
A sharp intake.
A careless disregard,
and they're gone.

Now the first wisp begins to curl,
rising to grey,
higher, thicker.
The blades of grass turn in alarm
as the flames take hold,
flickering, intensifying
until the grass
wilts in submission.
The flowers' colours
char, singe, scorch.
The treetops choke,
roots withered to claws.

This is the sight that greets me:
a garden annihilated.
Dead.
Black.
Utterly devastated.
I leave.

Yet the sun still rises and sets
over and over.
The rain falls
over and over.
Seasons pass
until one tender shoot
peeks up from the earth,
beckoning others to follow
in dots and lines and swathes.
Flowers detonate their colours
here and there and here.
Trees once more turn their heads to the busy dance of
butterflies,
bees,
birds,
life
returning to a garden.
I can't believe my eyes.

TMI SLI?

Sometimes I wonder: do my interpreters know me too
well?
Where do we draw the line?
I know they have professional boundaries,
but where do I draw mine?

Working in theatre and backstage,
terps have seen me in my drawers,
and when my belt got caught in my knickers
one nearly saw a lot more…

They've seen me nervous backstage;
they've seen me psych myself up.
And when I've cocked up a poem,
they've seen me beat myself up.

After an energetic rehearsal,
I queried if my new bra was up to the task.
The director, techie and co-star were all men;
who else was I going to ask?

I've asked them if my eczema was improving.
I've wiped my glasses on an interpreter's dress.
I've asked them to hold things for me for a minute.
These things, and more, I confess.

They've seen me coming off my medication,
the lows of antidepressant withdrawal.
They've been there for awards and post-shows,
the highs when I'm having a ball.

They've also been there in the dark moments,
translating the diagnosis on my eyes
or relaying the loss of my high pitches.
Interpreters have seen me cry.

Interpreters have seen me annoyed,
happy, excited, sad.
And, genuinely, sometimes I wonder
if I'm the weirdest client they've had.

But the thing I wonder most of all
is where should we draw that line?
Maybe it's case-by-case, but still…
when is it TMI SLI?

MY CAT

My cat.
                              Old?
                              Time to go?
Passed on.

Time went by.
Missing feline company.
Heart ready.
Went to cat home.
Looked around.

First cat…   licked its arse.

Second cat…   whoa!

Third cat…   dreaming mayhem.

Suddenly,
a lively kitten.
Our eyes met.
Beautiful! White fur all over! Aww.
No, too much, too hyper, too young, too…

What's that?

It's deaf?

That's *my* cat.

THE DEVIL CAT

To the bemused (non-signing) audience member
watching a heartfelt rendition of 'My Cat' in BSL,
my ears were my horns;
my teeth were extra sharp,
as sharp as my pitchfork claws.
My tail was a mark of the devil;
I was the devil cat.

So shall I am, so shall I do…
in the deepest, darkest corner,
where they'll never find it.

I'll hunt innocent insects,
regardless of consequences
for the innocent favourite rug.

I'll find the most thoughtful presents,
decorated with red and guts,
and be confused by the rejection.

I'll get my revenge by waiting
until my human passes by:
a sudden dash, a trip, they'll fly!

What's this? A shotgun exorcism…?
I may have lost a life…
I have eight more!

CAN YOU HEAR ME NOW?

Inspired by Jasmine Cooray's poem 'Examinations'.

Can you please look towards the window
and turn around if you hear something?

Can you lipread?
I can't be bothered to try harder

to communicate with you. I'm sure
you can understand me if you just try harder.

Please describe how your deafness affects your day-to-
day life.
Please describe how other people affect your day-to-day
life.

How about now? Yes, I know
covering my mouth is a dick move;

you're supposed to laugh –
this is a funny joke

at your expense. Can you hear me yet?
You speak so well;

why do you need interpreters?
You speak too well;

you can't be deaf.
You raised mainstream?

You're not Deaf enough.
Press the button when you hear the beep.

So many lip patterns; you look hearing.
Oh, I didn't realise; you don't look deaf.

Please provide a copy
of your most recent audiogram.

BLOOD

A tribute to those from the deaf community who have lost their lives to suicide.

Depression   Financial barriers
Internal wounds   External cuts

Bleeding out

THIS IS HOW I SIGN MY SONG

My singing voice is terrible.
It's flat, it's tuneless, too quiet, too loud.
Deaf to my own pitch, volume, tones;
others tell me how it sounds
when I sing.
Usually, they beg me to stop.
Nobody wants to listen
to me singing
my song, or any song;
my discordant keys
and broken, dissonant harmonies
don't belong.
Do they not see
how I sing my song?
My hands weave
my melodies;
my fingers strum
the notes I hum.
My face, my eyes,
my hands, my sighs
express emotion
as much as any
power ballad.
My lyrics, my rhythms
in three dimensions,
my song in signs
surely just as
if not more valid?
This is how I sign my song,
if they'd only listen.

REQUIEM FOR KATE MCKENZIE

Inspired by Last Tango in Halifax.

From the very first scene that I saw her,
I couldn't believe what I was seeing.
A smiling lesbian!
Comfortable in her identity,
good job, great prospects, beautiful girlfriend.
Is this possible? Apparently, yes!

Of course, there were problems to negotiate.
Said girlfriend was a nervous wreck
with a battleaxe of a mother
and a nightmare ex.
Through two series, I rooted for Kate
as she fought for Caroline,
for love, against hate.

She helped Caroline conquer fear:
other people's, her students', her own.
Having endured and eventually tiring
of Caroline's self-destructive crap,
Kate's act of self-respect, self-preservation
gave a much-needed realisation.

And, finally forgiving, she came back!
And they danced
and they kissed
and I sniffled
and I cheered.
She got her happy ending.
I got my happy ending.

I couldn't wait for the next series!
A well-educated, erudite, successful lesbian
as a main character: bring it on!

No doubt there'd be hilarious misunderstandings
and ups and downs and, for the finale,
maybe Celia the battleaxe
would finally accept Kate and her beautiful grandbaby
and join the twenty-first century at long last.
So many rich narrative seams just waiting to be explor—

screech, crash.

Now forever untapped.

Now Caroline's
childish, homophobic bitch mother,
who never approved from the start,
faces no consequences
for breaking her daughter's heart.

No chance for redemption
for abstaining the dream wedding,
for shunning Caroline's pregnant partner,
for her unthinking, ignorant meddling.

Never mind Kate's American mother,
phoning in from across the lake,
chatting calmly
with her daughter's wife's ex
about his vacuous novels
at her daughter's wake

while the aforementioned bitch
spent her time not comforting
anyone
but harassing
her poor husband Alan
for having a single, soothing cigarette.

Why not throw John under the bus?
Or Lawrence, who referred to the baby as 'it'?
Instead of getting rid of wonderful Kate,
get rid of the insensitive little shit.
Apparently it was a narrative decision
to introduce death in a comedy-drama.
Apparently so Caroline and Celia
could make up in the aftermath.
I'll have to presume Kate crashed the car
in a suitably tragi-comic way.

I cried through the funeral,
hoping for a twist,
or that it was a mistake,
or, at the very least,
John would fall into the grave
and break his neck.

As my favourite character –
hell, the only
completely likable character –
was laid to rest,
so, for me,
was *Last Tango in Halifax*.

The only way the show could be redeemed
would be if it retconned the entire third series
and did a *Dallas*.

I'll even help with the first scene.
Fade in
to a shot of a shower cubicle,
glass sides steamed up,
a figure vaguely visible within.
Cut to Caroline in the shower
(shoulders and above only,
just for good taste).
A look of concern crosses her face.

Suddenly, the shower door opens.
Kate appears.
She asks if everything is all right.
Caroline smiles
and says she just had a bad dream.
Kate smiles
and offers to make it all better.

Cut back to even more steamed-up glass
as the door closes
and the barely-visible figures within embrace.
I'd watch that.
Hell, I don't know anybody who wouldn't watch that.

Until then,
goodbye, *Last Tango in Halifax,*
and rest in peace,
Kate McKenzie.

TO MY TWENTY-THREE-YEAR-OLD SELF

Get out of that bed.
Actually, no – stay in it.
Heck knows
it's not an option you're going to have a few years from
now.
Enjoy it while you can.
Get back in that bed.

Get those pills.
It's not normal to feel that bad about yourself.
Get down to the GP. Ask for help.
Don't listen to those who say pills aren't the answer.
For you, they are.
Get the pills.

'Poet' *is* a job title.
You can be a professional poet.
People will pay you to perform poetry. Yes, they will.
It does mean you'll have to deal with people… and all
that entails.
You can do it.
You *can* be a poet.

Don't accept gigs for exposure
or as a favour for friends.
Exposure will not pay the bills or feed the cats.
Friends can and will dick you over,
and you'll never speak to them again.
Your work and your friendships are worth more.

Don't listen to that little voice –
the one in your head
that tells you this is rubbish and no one will care,

or, in your darkest moments, that you're better off dead.
In fact, drag it out, throw it down
and stamp on it as hard as you can.
It's not going to be easy.
Nothing ever is.
You're going to make mistakes.
Everyone does.
There is no shame
in doing your best.

I changed my mind.
Get out of that bed.

SIGNS ARE LIVING, BREATHING

What is a Sign Language poem?
It's a living, moving thing.
My hands dance in air;
the Signs flow and sing.

My face gives all away;
am I happy, excited, sad?
My body emphasises,
was this thing good or bad?

A poem on the page
with words prettily aligned
has its own skill and beauty,
but it's not the same as Sign.

Words are static, unmoving,
dead, laid out for all to see.
Signs are living, breathing;
my poems live in me.

I know what I want to say;
in Sign, it's so clear,
but writing down my poems
can fill me with fear.

I want to create on paper
what I see in my mind,
but, no matter how good the word,
it'll never be a Sign.

The Signs struggle and resist,
their meanings captured in a page.
They lie there, sullen, defeated;
they know they look better on a stage.

Words are static, unmoving.
Dead, laid out for all to see.
Signs are living, breathing;
my poems live in me.

TO THE UNREPENTANT DRINK DRIVER

Wedding guests gathered:
drinks and chat,
bubbles and cake,
light and relaxed.
Refreshments all round
and stories are shared:
how we know the happy couple,
histories compared.
Among us, an Aussie,
apparently an old friend,
charming and affable.
I didn't comprehend
just how much he was going to offend.

Someone asks
if it's true what they say:
do Australians really
drink all day?
Yes, he laughs,
booze culture is strong;
the Aussies can carouse
all day long.
There's chuckles and smiles,
but then it takes a turn
as he confesses
without apparent concern
something that makes my composure churn.

How back in the day
he'd take his car
and go for a drink
in the local bars.
He'd get hammered
and then
he'd drive his car
home again.
Stillness descends.

Someone else politely suggests (how British!)
that he could have come to strife;
that maybe his actions
could have changed someone's life.
The answer – a nonchalant shrug,
an indifferent wave of the hand.
For moment I'm stuck in the sand
of shock.
What should I say?
I don't want to ruin this lovely day.

Still, I remember:
the grief of friends,
their loved ones' lives
brought to an end.
And the time in my village
when a drunken young man
and one of his passengers
were killed.
He'd flown his car down a local hill,
heedless of the junction
up ahead,
traffic lights red.

Flowers are left there
to this day.
That's what I really
wanted to say.
Yet as I stared
at the blithe disregard,
blinded by the arrogance,
the moment passed…
but afterwards, I wished I'd asked…

if you'd ever really thought it through,

the potential harm that you could do?

Maybe one day, I'll say this to you.

MY SIN

I confess my sin.
My sin is envy.
Don't get me wrong;
I wouldn't be anyone else.
I'm quite happy.

But once in a while I get…

Male envy.
When they can just whip it out
and pee where they like
and reach the tallest shelves
with their annoying height.

Straight envy.
When I see hetero couples walk down the street hand in
hand,
doing little PDAs without a second thought:
is anyone looking? What's this area like? Can they tell
we're
        both women?
Is this a battle that needs to be fought?

Able-bodied envy.
Watching people skip across the road against the lights
and prance up and down some steps
without any fear of a rebellious knee or inner ear
and falling down and breaking their necks.

Hearing envy.
They can go where they like, watch what they like, when
they like.
They don't get pushed aside or given filthy looks
for 'ignoring' excuse-mes. They know the train is late,
or the gate has changed, without even having to look.

Muggle envy.
This one's more about curiosity,
because I'm just not aware…
what must it be like to know a film has made a complete
mess
        of a book
and genuinely not care?

I DON'T WANT CONSENT (I WANT ENTHUSIASM)

An Anton de Firefly poem. Anton de Firefly is my drag king alter-ego.

I don't want consent;
I want enthusiasm!
I want to stop with exhaustion
after the ninth orgasm.

I don't want someone who looks at me
and mumbles, 'All right, I guess…'
I want someone who swoons and screams,
'Yes! A hundred times, yes!'

I don't want to do all the chasing,
not with the state of my knees.
At the same time, I'd appreciate:
if I say no, don't chase me!

I don't want to be kissed
with a bored, uninterested sigh.
I want to be kissed such that I forget…
where was I?

I don't want to hold someone down –
unless it's one of their kinks.
I like to think I'm open-minded…
though I draw the line at whips.

If someone says, 'No, thanks,
you're not the one for me.'
I'll smile and say, 'No problem;
there's plenty more fish in the sea.'

If someone's not that interested,
I'm not interested either.
There's many ways to express affection;
in cuddling, I'm a believer.

I don't want to do all the work;
I want equal participation.
I want a mutual enterprise,
not mere capitulation.

That's why I don't want consent;
I want enthusiasm.
I want romance and hearts and flowers
and – if they want – red-hot passion!

NO LONGER AN IMPOSSIBLE DREAM

*Originally printed in QDA: A Queer Disability Anthology,
edited by Raymond Luczak (Squares & Rebels, 2015).*

I want to be proposed to;
I want to be swept away
like in those YouTube videos.
There doesn't have to be a DJ
or a marching band
and they don't necessarily
have to learn to dance,
so long as there's signs,
big bits of paper or a BSL song
or creative use of a Jumbotron,
but whatever they do,
I want to be impressed
and be overwhelmed with love
as I tearfully say yes.
My ring would be silver with Gallifreyan script,
or notated Signs,
or inspired by *Thrones*,
or *Discworld*-designed;
no need for stones.
Well, maybe something blue,
a lazuli or two,
and it would be
a heart-melting gift.
I would wear a suit
or a shirt and boards.
I'd like to do it on a beach,
preferably abroad,
but nothing so soppy
as an arch,
especially not wrapped with roses;
that would just be too much.

Simple vows, nothing gushy;
we'll have the poems
getting mushy,
and the whole thing would be
a bilingual treat.
There'd be palm trees and a fresh breeze,
white sands and turquoise seas,
with just a few friends
and her and me.

Inspired by recognition of same-sex marriage in the UK in 2014.

ALL THAT HISSES…

Beautiful patterns of fur.
Gorgeous eyes and lulling purr.
An incautious hand.

WHEN THE DEAD ARE CURED

Zombies surround me:
bodies, faces say nothing.
Only their mouths move.

They communicate
with lips, teeth, tongue, flapping around.
Their bodies are dead.

I am surrounded,
outnumbered, overwhelmed.
But not defeated.

I seek out survivors;
we erect the barricades.
Keep the cold ones out.

Our bodies are alive,
our hands, our faces, our eyes.
We are warmed by Signs.

The dead walk on outside
and tell us we are broken.
Oh, for a majority!

Or a flamethrower – of Signs,
to drown the zombies in heat
until their bodies live.

Hands twitching, awaken,
expressions of joy, delight.
Look! A miracle!

When the dead are cured,
and they know the warmth of Signs,
the world will be saved.

A LIFESTYLE CHOICE

Apparently I made
a lifestyle choice.

To be deaf,
to be depressed,
to be queer,
to be different.

My choice
was to stop hiding.

BUBBLE BURST

In the top front row
of a city sightseeing bus
on a dark evening,
the woman next to me
wearing the tour earbuds
signing the landmarks.
Me holding the official map,
matching numbers.
Landmark 17, stop 3;
this cathedral was built in the eighteenth century.
Pertinent facts and warm gazes.
Smiling corrections
and learning of new signs.
Teaching my language
and learning hers.
Snuggling close against
the cold night air.
A special evening
and memory;
a happy, harmless bubble.
A little while ago,
my bubble burst
on a dark night
in the top front row
of a city bus.

Inspired by a news story of two women on a date, who were on the top front row of a bus when they were beaten up in a homophobic attack.

WHAT IS THE WORTH OF MY LIFE?

What is the worth of my life?
How should this be defined?
By the labour of my body
or the labour of my mind?

Should it be by my burden,
my cost to the welfare state?
Should I tally up my expenses
and see if the figures equate?

The cost of midwives at my birth,
who freed my strangling cord;
my very first operation,
my care on the paediatric ward?

Or the cost of my second operation,
when I was seven, to save my sight?
Breaking the stitches on my eyeball
must have affected the price.

Or the surgeries on my foot?
Wasted money, I'm sorry to say.
Stubborn body piling on the expenses,
since I'll claim Motability someday.

Let's not forget audiology.
I can't imagine the bill so far.
Suffice to say, these aids alone
could buy me a brand new car.

The financial product of my labours
fails the test of the balance sheet.
Unless I become a rich poet(!),
my costs I can't begin to meet.

So how do I define my worth?
I judge it by the worth of my days.
I've travelled to three other continents;
I was Queen of the Birds in a play.

I'm a carer for my elderly parents,
I have two university degrees,
I'm training to be a translator,
but are the various aids all anybody sees?

Poems have shown me the world
and worlds beside my own,
helped me see through the eyes of others
and understand that I am not alone.

So my message to the eugenicists
and to the Daily Heil:
judge us not by what it costs to sustain us,
but how we make our lives worthwhile.

IT WAS ON FACEBOOK

Best performed live with an audience joining in on the chorus.

Oh my gosh, I am so sorry.
I didn't know your dog was dying.
Why didn't you say something?
I could have come to say goodbye.

'It was on Facebook.'

What do you mean there was a scratch performance
of a brand new show
with deaf and hearing actors when I was in town?
How come I didn't know?

'It was on Facebook.'

Oh no, I am so sorry.
I had no idea. Are you OK?
I wouldn't have asked if I'd known he was in prison
or that you had to have him put away.

'It was on Facebook.'

Why didn't you tell me there was a poetry workshop
with BSL interpreters, no less?
Seriously, why didn't you say something?
I know you have my email address.

'It was on Facebook.'

Oh my word, I am so sorry.
I didn't realise you'd been so ill.
Why didn't you text? I'd have come to visit.
I'd have brought grapes or picked up some pills.

'It was on Facebook.'
When did we swap the word 'human'
for an 'internet' or 'social' connection?
If you have big news, please just tell me,
and please don't say, when it comes to my attention,

'It was on Facebook!'

IT WAS JUST KIDS

'It was just kids being kids.'

It's funny
how high school misery
can so easily
be dismissed.
Had we all been adults,
the law forbids…

Any act by which a person intentionally
or recklessly
causes another
to suffer
or apprehend immediate unlawful violence.

    Ah, so ambushing someone
    at the school gates
    and shoving a snowball in their face
    would be an arrestable offence.
    Fancy that.

A course of conduct which amounts
to harassment of another
and which he knows
or ought to know
amounts to harassment of the other.

    They knew.
    They definitely knew.

Whosoever shall unlawfully
and maliciously
inflict any grievous bodily harm
on any other person,
either with or without a weapon or instrument.

    Does a flight of stairs count as an instrument?

At least I grabbed the bannister
when I felt the push.
Hanging on, I turned and looked into a laughing face.
So. Funny.

Unwanted verbal, non-verbal or physical conduct
of a sexual nature
which has the purpose or effect
of violating the recipient's dignity,
or of creating an intimidating,
hostile,
degrading,
humiliating
or offensive environment for the recipient.

I suppose some people would argue:
hundreds of teenagers in the same place,
what do you expect?
Not the page from a softcore mag
stuffed in my bag
that's for sure.

Why does it seem to be accepted
that if you're different,
school can be shit?
At the time, I thought it was normal,
but now when I think of it…
I find myself fantasising:

instead of high school, a courtroom.
Instead of 'it was just kids being kids':
common assault,
harassment,
attempted GBH,
sexual harassment
and actual consequences.

But for some reason,
because this happened at school,
it's OK.
It was just kids being kids.

PALLAS ATHENE

Commission for Royal Collection, November 2020.

Shyly averting my gaze
as people pass by,
an unassuming beauty
for an unassuming eye.
Myths and legends
of cunning and vengeance belie.
One day I might
look

SIGNS OF LIFE

Commission for Deaf Explorer, April 2021.

This poem is alive
where the written word
is static and hollow.

My signs breathe life
into this verse.

This poem has a beat,
a pulsing rhythm,
signs dancing in cadence.

Signs traverse our differences,
common signals traced by lines.

This poem articulates emotion;
my body, my face show all.

Compare this to static words;

paper cannot breathe,
words have no pulse,
text has no spark of life,
no face to show a feeling.

Compare this poor page
to the riches and vitality
of Sign!

THE SURDOGRAM (OR: I SEE YOU)

If you've ever felt like giving up on group conversations entirely… you're deaf.

If you've felt like giving up on hearing people entirely… you're deaf.

If you've missed an appointment because you didn't hear someone calling your name… you're deaf.

If you've struggled to understand someone because they were standing in front of the light… you're deaf.

If you've missed a train because you didn't hear the tannoy announcing a platform change and it didn't show up on the screens… you're deaf.

If people who should know better have repeatedly called you despite your repeated, repeated, repeated requests not to do so… you're deaf.

If you've been hit with a shopping trolley because you didn't hear someone say, 'Excuse me? Excuse me?!'… you're deaf.

If you've wondered what the hell everyone is laughing at and worried it might be you… you're deaf.

If you've been punched because you didn't hear someone yelling at you that you were in their seat… you're deaf.

There's no need to display your big 'D';
this gate is open, drive on through.
If the hearing-centric,
hearing-obsessed
hearing world
has stiffed you somehow,
I see you.
You're deaf.
Like me.

I KNOW SIGN LANGUAGE!

A is a digit of doom –
B looks for exits in the room.
C is communication reduced to a crawl.
D is for cool, not.
E is eye strain.
F is for F…
G is a frustrated growl.
Hi there!
I know sign language!
Just
KilL
Me
Now.
O needs a count and an encouraging smile.
P looks like a D, but we're nearly there.
Q – a handy perch for a hanging rope…
R dangles precariously.
S is always a struggle…
T is for who told you this was OK?
U is the last vowel but… still needs a count?
V is for violence, against your teacher,
Who clearly never warned you not to do this.
X quickens to the end in sight.
Y does no one ever get this one right?
Zzzzz… finally!

Well done, you know the alphabet!
When are you going to learn

MELANCHOLY VILLANELLE

There are times when I'd rather lie in bed,
burrow down and hide from light of day,
pretending to all the world I'm dead.

Days that are the day before retread,
greys turning greyer into yet more grey:
there are times when I'd rather lie in bed.

When there's only bitterness in my head,
futility bids me lifeless stay,
pretending to all the world I'm dead.

When the wings of melancholy spread,
spying distant hope as its prey,
there are times when I'd rather lie in bed.

When every thought is tinged with dread,
let me under covers be cast away,
pretending to all the world I'm dead.

When my sanity is held by only a thread,
and that thread seems ready to fray,
there are times when I'd rather lie in bed,
pretending to all the world I'm dead.

MUDDLED MUSINGS

Those who believe as I do
we must, however, acknowledge
an embryo with a known defect
as it seems to me
that the production of a defective race
man with all his noble qualities
human beings
shall not be preferred
yet still bears in his bodily frame
a great calamity to the world
over an embryo
examine carefully
the indelible stamp
the causes
of his lowly origin
intermarriage
without that known defect
with the object of applying a remedy
of the deaf.

Original quotes:

*'An embryo with a known defect shall not be preferred
over an embryo without that known defect.'*
Clause 14, Human Fertilisation and Embryology
(Amendments) Act 2008. Original explanatory notes
mentioned deafness as a condition that could be
targeted; notes were removed after protests from the
deaf community

'We must, however, acknowledge, as it seems to me, that man with all his noble qualities … still bears in his bodily frame the indelible stamp of his lowly origin.'

Charles Darwin

'Those who believe as I do, that the production of a defective race of human beings would be a great calamity to the world, will examine carefully the causes of that which will lead to intermarriage of the deaf with the object of applying a remedy.'

Alexander Graham Bell

THE BIRDS

The birds are tweeting again.
Not clickbait fake-news tweets
but loud, piercing ack-ack-acks
and cheep-chirrup-cheeps
and dur-dur-dums and trills
as harsh as the most
ignorant and hate-filled
tweets.
When hearing people talk
about what the deaf are missing,
guaranteed they'll mention birdsong.
What a lie.
Birds don't sing.
Birdsong implies a melody,
intent, cohesion,
musical ability.
An orchestra working together.
Rather, the birds in my garden
vociferously tweet over each other
with as much fervour
and passion
as a particularly hostile
Twitter war,
one that begins anew
with each rising of the sun.
What this lot need is a conductor.
What I need is a gun.

BUDDING ENBY

When I was a baby
wearing a pink frilly hat,
people asked my parents,
'What's his name?'
Apparently my gender
was ambiguous even then.
It wasn't fair that boys
had cooler clothes,
got better toys.
Who wants to wear leggings
and play with dolls?
I never wanted to kiss the boys
or gossip about them.
I just wanted to be allowed
to kick the ball.

BEACH POEM BY NUMBERS

I'm sat on a beach knitting a scarf.
It's a beautiful day.
Warm sun and soft sand,
waves rumbling nearby.
Clear skies complement blue seas and pale shores,
gentle breezes wafting of seaweed and salt.
I'm far from home.
When this day is past
and I'm long home,
bitter breezes wafting of iron and storms
to complement grey skies and greyer streets
and rumbling thunder,
I'll wear warm, soft wool
and remember the day
I sat on a beach knitting a scarf.

BETTER DEAF THAN DEAD

Why can't people think instead?
'I'd rather be dead than deaf,' they write;
I'd rather be deaf than dead.

Would their lives be such a plight,
so unbearable, so lacking worth?
'I'd rather be dead than deaf,' they write.

They'd wish away their time on Earth,
for, without sound, would their lives be
so unbearable, so lacking worth?

Spared some of life's cacophony,
is there no bright side to be found?
For, without sound, would their lives be

just as worthwhile and profound?
Does one need noise to appreciate life?
Is there no bright side to be found?

Given the preciousness of life,
why can't people think instead,
one doesn't need noise to appreciate life;
I'd rather be deaf than dead.

I WISH I COULD SAVE MY LIFE

Some scientists say
that maybe
we're just streams of consciousness
of code
in a grand simulation.
Maybe
it's all a game.

In that case,
I wish I could save my life;
touch a button,
see a message: *Your progress in life has been saved up to this point.*

Then it wouldn't matter
how many things I messed up,
how many things I forgot,
how many things I misheard,
how many things I tripped over,
how stupid I looked.

I could just press pause,
navigate to the menu,
find the saved file,
click load
and try again,
and this time do it *better.*

I wish I could save my life;
pause and take stock
and double-check
the walkthrough
that I bought on eBay
(it may or may not be a rip-off),

just to make sure I'm doing it right.
I'm probably doing it wrong.
At least this way
I can avoid the obvious mistakes:

obvious only if you've read the walkthrough
or you're not completely absent-minded
or if you can hear what's happening
and clues aren't hidden in the (spoken) (uncaptioned)
dialogue.

Like the ambush I kept walking into in *KOTOR*
because I couldn't hear the stormtroopers' radio.
Like all the trains I've missed because platform changes
were
              announced on the tannoy
but not on the bloody screens.
Like the time I got punched because I didn't hear someone
         saying (I presume)
'Excuse me… Excuse me? Excuse me?!'
(What's wrong with a tap on the shoulder? For goodness'
sake.)

I wish I could save my life;
take a break,
have a KitKat,
a fortifying sip of water
or something stronger…

I wish I could save my life;
take a break from being reasonable,
from politely advocating
for my rights to access,
to exist.
I'd activate my energy shield,
tool up with frag grenades,
load up my repeating blaster
and use the cheat code for unlimited ammo.

And shoot everything up;
blow it all to bits
and shoot what's left again.
I'd annihilate every last barrier
in a beautiful, glorious, devastating
orgy of destruction.

Game paused.
Do you wish to continue?

THE TRUE DEAFNESS

*'What matters deafness of the ear when the mind hears?
The true deafness, the incurable deafness, is deafness of
the mind.'*

Victor Hugo

Closed ears – immaterial.
Closed mind – incurable.

PRAY AWAY THE HAY

An Anton de Firefly poem.

Pray away the hay
in your head.
Think about what Jesus said:
love thy neighbour.
If God created the world and all that's in it
and has some fantastic plan…
doesn't that include you and me and all the other idiots?
Isn't he 'the man'?
Actually, while we're here: he?
God is an all-powerful, all-seeing metaphysical presence;
why does he have a gender? Shouldn't he be a they?
Hell, if they're all-powerful, they can be whatever they want.
Who are we mere mortals to assign a gender *to God*?

Pray away the hay,
if you could;
all that straw's doing you no good.
What's this 'Adam and Eve, not Adam and Steve'?
Adam and Eve had a choice of one!
Who's to say
they weren't gay – or bi?
It's not like they had a chance to try
any alternatives.
Which of the ten commandments
or the seven sins says
'Thou shalt not be fabulous'?

Pray away the hay
in your hair,
and if you really care
what God thinks,
then look within.
Before you cast that goddamned stone,
maybe atone.
We are none of us without sin,
and some of us
are just trying our best
to get from one day to the next,
and we want to try and make it a fabulous day…
why not join us?
And put those goddamned stones away.

A PANDEMIC TALISMAN

I don't have religion.
If pushed, I might say Jedi
or vaguely C of E.
There may have been a Christ,
but his holiness
was bestowed by holy men
who wanted to promote their holy book
amid an arena of pantheons,
of sprites, multi-limbed savants
and all-powerful lightning throwers.
Quite possibly
a more remarkable protagonist was needed
to capture the imagination of the masses.

Not for me a cross worn around the neck
or even a handheld one in my bag,
depicting some poor flogged bastard
who made the mistake of preaching love
in the wrong place at the wrong time,
to ward off impromptu vampire attacks.
Besides, the strange beasts that lurk about
wouldn't be repelled
by me waving around
intersected bits of wood,
though they might call the police.

Nor for me a lightsaber.
I'm liable to accidentally cut off a limb –
maybe my own –
and then where will I be?

No.
My talismans are more mundane.

Two simple badges pinned
on my official pandemic washable facemask.
These small round bits of metal
are my protective shield
against other people's ignorance.
These amulets carry a concise, magical message.
On seeing them,
reading them,
the uninformed
are informed
that I am special
and they are going to try harder
in this interaction
than they may have expected.
Poor lambs.
No longer do the words
'Can you lipread?'
signal
'Will you do all the work for me in this conversation?'
when said words are smothered
by cloth, paper, valves, plastic.

In a world where people jump from 'excuse me'
to sarcasm
to shouting
straight to a blow,
do not collect £100,
do not pass Go
or even indeed (gasp)
tap someone on the shoulder to get their attention –
no, let's hit them first –
instead of letting my temper burst
and condemning them to their nth generation cursed,
I seek prevention
and protection
in emblems with a caption.

Two mottos on the mask I wear.
In colourful characters they declare:

I'm deaf
and
I sign BSL.

THE PEN

The pen is mighty indeed.
Scribbled verses,
scrawlings of hate,
sweet nothings of love.
Bombastic notes of rhapsody
or quiet, soothing melodies.
Forge against injustice,
carefully word judgements,
spread rumours,
sow discord,
spark a revolution:
a thesis nailed to a door.
Cards of condolence,
birthday wishes,
get-well-soons,
round robins.
Little 'just saw this and thought of you's,
or a new scientific breakthrough.
Or the everyday:
bananas, bread, eggs,
don't forget the toothpaste.
To whom it may concern,
I write to complain,
with best wishes,
your faithful servant.
What pity, then,
when the fire that fuels the pen
dies out.

INTERDIMENSIONAL TRAVELLER

I have a passport
of sorts.
The cover has an emblem
of a multiple Venn diagram
with a sketch of an open hand
in the central,
many-times-overlapped
novel shape.

With it, I navigate spaces,
cross ephemeral borders,
visit strange worlds with strange languages
and even stranger inhabitants.
I have no TARDIS,
yet I traverse dimensions.

2D planes of paper and words,
3D spheres of movement and signs,
the fourth dimension
of the time
it takes to move a hand
from here
                to there.
Endless zooms warping 3D
into 2D.
Unfolding focal fatigue.

I travel through time,
or maybe it just seems that way
when the same old shit happens
time and time again.
Barriers unyielding,
defended by the ignorant,

braced by antiquated
automated
telephone systems.
My passport may not be recognised everywhere.
Nevertheless,
I wander through dimensions,
margins and lines
more blurred
every time.

WHO AM I? (Finished 2008, occasionally updated)

Who am I?
Raised in hearing culture

Late… found deaf culture
Hearing identity have

Deaf identity have
Both absorbed
But they grind and fracture

Who am I?
In the hearing world
I'm labelled 'hearing-impaired'
'Broken'… 'damaged'

In the Deaf world
I'm labelled 'speaks well'
'Half-hearing'… 'oral'

I can speak
But do I fit in the hearing world?
Sometimes…

I can sign
But do I fit in the Deaf world?
Sometimes…

Half-hearing

Half-deaf
Together becomes what?
Who am I?

Introspection

Deaf
	Hearing
		Woman
			Queer
				Androgynous
				Geek
					Traveller
					My love of language
				And so on
					And on

		All of these identities and passions
		I see them all, and they're all part of me

				Acceptance

				Language
				Traveller
			Geek
			Androgynous
		Queer
		Woman
	Hearing
Deaf

			At last, it all clicks into place
That's who I am

Films of several of the poems are featured on the Sign Metaphor YouTube channel linked via this QR code or at: https://www.youtube.com/user/signmetaphor/videos

URLs for the other QR Codes are:
Bilingual Poet's Dilemma
https://www.scottishpoetrylibrary.org.uk/poem/bilingual-poets-dilemma/
Finally, A Dream Come True
https://vimeo.com/150103141
Pallas Athene
https://vimeo.com/654060355
Bella's Penguins
https://www.youtube.com/watch?v=edE5AZaeVo0
The Apple
https://www.youtube.com/watch?v=3XDlkdJ6o8o
Red and Green
https://www.youtube.com/watch?v=O_Baj81Vr7k
Phoenix Garden
https://www.youtube.com/watch?v=P-EVgeS0pLQ
My Cat
https://www.youtube.com/watch?v=Z7elrYoAFvs
That Day
https://www.youtube.com/watch?v=JsuGSFOx33w
The Duck and the Dissertation
https://www.youtube.com/watch?v=CbsblW77ytl&t=1s

ACKNOWLDEGMENTS

Martin Haswell - filmed and edited No Longer An Impossible Dream / Finally A Dream Come True
San Alland - directed and edited A Bilingual Poet's Dilemma
Rachel Sutton-Spence - granted permission to use links from Sign Metaphor YouTube channel

Thanks:
To my Mother, for her unwavering support and faith in me.
To all the friends who've been there over the years.
To my cats, just because.

9 781913 958114